TRANS AFFIRMATION COLORING BOOK

drawn and written by
Theo Nicole Lorenz

ISBN 978-0-9975738-3-1

My gender identity is one of the many lovable things about me.

My anger is valuable.

My gender presentation is for me,
and it can be whatever I want it to be.

I am the only one who gets to define me.

I am enough exactly as I am.

I deserve to feel happy, safe, and loved.

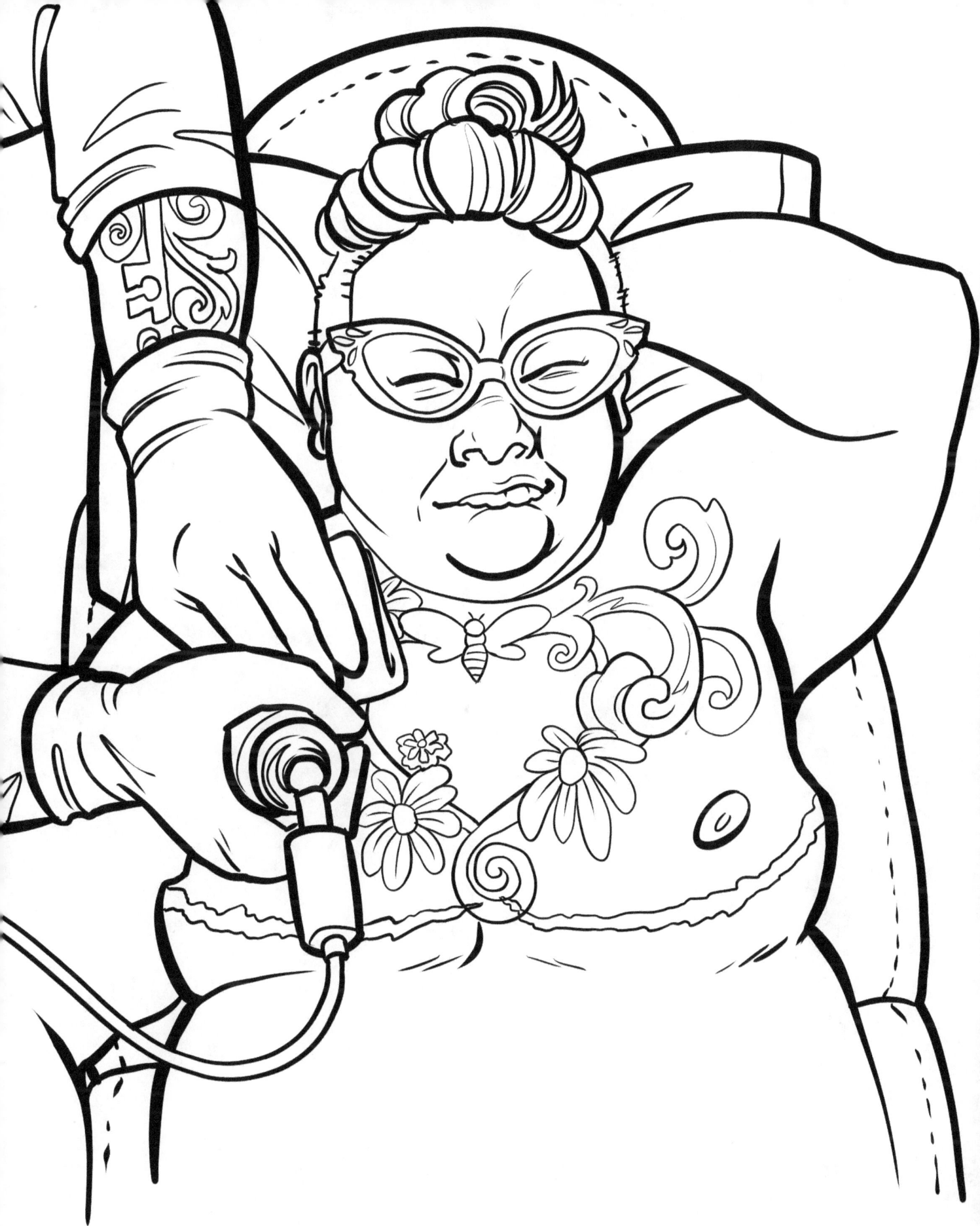

My body is mine and I will make it my home.

I am not alone.

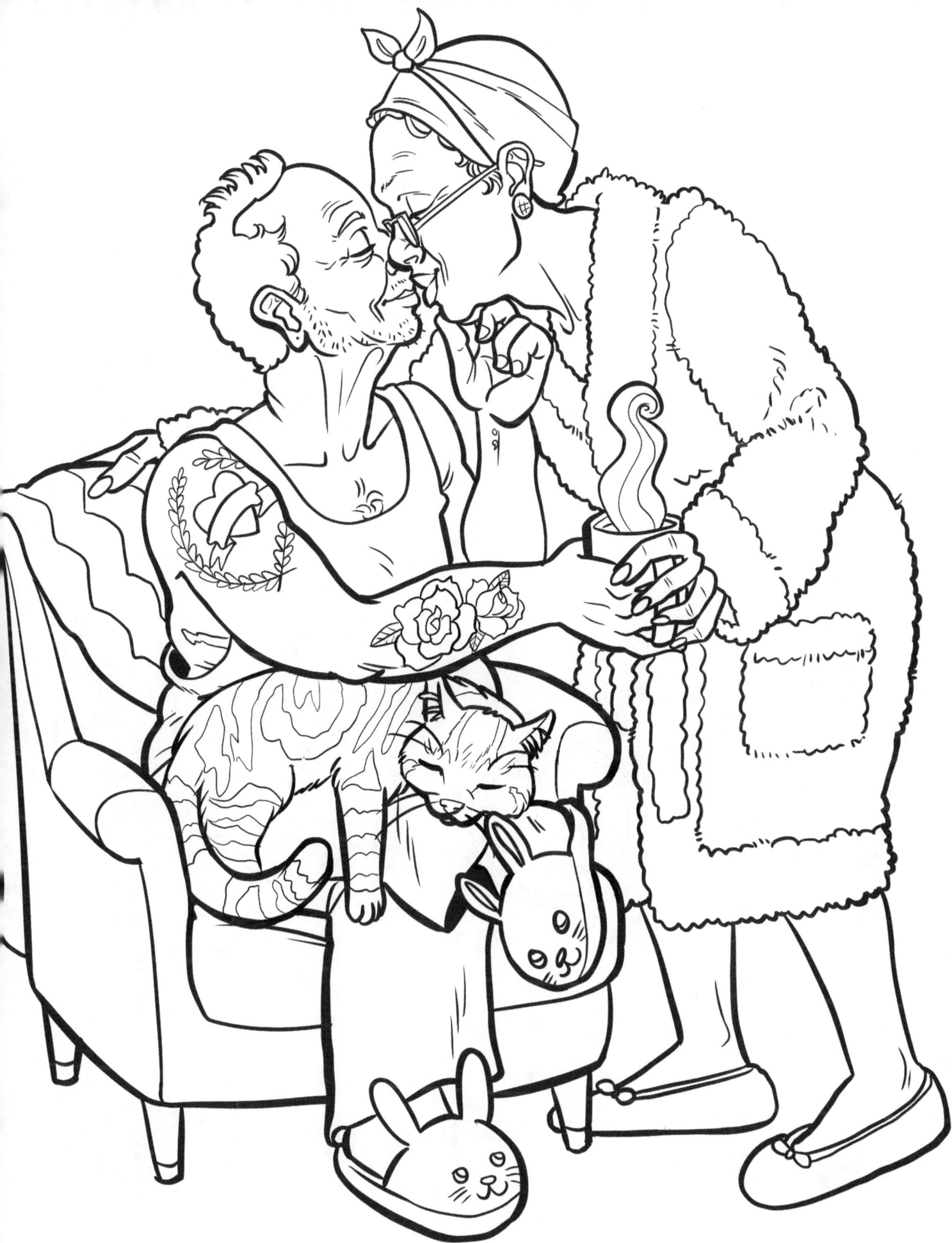

We're trans, and we're not going anywhere.

The Trans Affirmation Coloring Book Worksheet

I am lovable and I deserve to be here. This page is for me to fill out and read when I need to be reminded of that.

Here are 5 things I can do that usually make me feel better:

1.

2.

3.

4.

5.

Here are 3 people who love me and ways I can reach them when I need to talk to someone:

1.

2.

3.

Here are some resources I can reach out to if I need help:

Trans Lifeline US: 877-565-8860 (Canada: 877-330-6366)

The Trevor Project 866-488-7386
Chat and text help: thetrevorproject.org/get-help-now

About the Artist

Theo is a non-binary trans writer and artist who lives with their partner (who is also trans), a young step-son who's currently obsessed with princesses and explosions, and too many cats in Saint Paul, Minnesota.

Theo makes coloring books like Unicorns Are Jerks, Dinosaurs With Jobs, and WHY CAT WHY.
Check out more of their work at TheoNicole.com.